FROM HERO TO ZERO
AND
BACK AGAIN!

By Wil Lovelock

Published 2009 by arima publishing
www.arimapublishing.com

ISBN 978 1 84549 383 7

© Wil Lovelock 2009

All rights reserved

This book is copyright. Subject to statutory exception and to provisions of relevant collective licensing agreements, no part of this publication may be reproduced, stored in a retrieval system, or transmitted in any form or by any means, without the prior written permission of the author.

Printed and bound in the United Kingdom

Typeset in Palatino Linotype 14/16

This book is sold subject to the conditions that it shall not, by way of trade or otherwise, be lent, re-sold, hired out, or otherwise circulated without the publisher's prior consent in any form of binding or cover other than that which it is published and without a similar condition including this condition being imposed on the subsequent purchaser.

Swirl is an imprint of arima publishing.

arima publishing
ASK House, Northgate Avenue
Bury St Edmunds, Suffolk IP32 6BB
t: (+44) 01284 700321
www.arimapublishing.com

FOR GRUG AND ANNES

We are all born heroes; it's time to start acting like one...

Hero *n. one greatly regarded for achievements or qualities.*

Collins Gem – English dictionary

Zero *n. the lowest point.*

Collins Gem – English dictionary

CONTENTS

1. You were born a hero — 1

2. Forgetting who we are — 9

3. Heroes just know — 15

4. What is our hero? — 23

5. Finding the 'hero within' — 25

6. Launching the 'hero within' — 43

7. Super-Hero — 53

8. A brief trip back to zero — 63

9. The author's story — 69

You were born a hero...

At the moment of your creation, you were the sole survivor of 280,000,000 sperm* all swimming to reach that egg and you did it!

Maybe nobody has ever mentioned it but that was one impressive achievement and you can definitely have a high regard for achievements and qualities at that point in your life and in particular - your swimming!

You see, you were born a hero and if you can just remember how to behave like one, you can and will be one again.

Another fine quality you possessed at that point, was selflessness. Working (swimming) to your maximum ability in order to continue the human race (reach your goal) despite the potential risks to your own creation.

They were 280,000,000 to 1 odds and you weighed up the pros and cons, took the risk and were very successful if you don't mind me saying so!
And it doesn't stop there!

Once you had dutifully fertilised that egg, you became one with it and as you grew inside your mother's womb, you survived still more threats to your very being.

Great qualities – and still so young!

Then of course, came your entry into this strange and wonderful world. This itself came with great risk but in true hero fashion – you survived!

Source. Dr. Lindemann's sperm facts

FROM HERO TO ZERO AND BACK AGAIN!

So,

YOU beat 279,999,999 sperm to the finishing post.

YOU survived the constant threats to your very existence as you grew in your mother's womb.

YOU survived the trauma of childbirth.

YOU were born against the odds

And you are greatly admired for these achievements!

You are a hero!

Now that I have explained the basic reasons why I consider you and me both heroes, I will try to enlighten you a little further.
(If of course, you are not already convinced)

Up until now, your admirable qualities have been automatic. In other words, you weren't aware of being like or acting like a hero. You didn't care about being 'greatly regarded for your achievements or qualities'. You were just being! No thought processes, pride or lack of self- esteem to get in the way.

Now, as we move into the early weeks and months of our lives, we become more aware of the world around us and in particular, our need to interact with other human beings.

We are now 'cooking on gas' as far as being a hero is concerned. Greatly regarded for our little hands and podgy faces and our ability to bring up wind or fill a nappy. We are true heroes in every sense of our definition.

Our qualities and achievements really do make us little heroes and we're still not trying!

Moving on a little further in our early existence and we're learning new skills daily. We sit up, we stand, we walk and we fall down. Not a negative comment should we receive, as of course, we are trying and often succeeding and we are highly regarded for these qualities and achievements also.

Step into young childhood itself and our abilities to achieve and show off our great qualities are endless. We learn to swim (again), kick a ball, read a book, sing, dance, ride a bike and so much more. We still fall down on a regular basis but it is our ability to get back up again for which we are most greatly regarded.

Our teenage years, though complicated, offer us still more opportunities to live like heroes. We become more independent, responsible, achieve better skills and qualifications and are preparing ourselves to be the true heroes of the adult world.

'GREATLY REGARDED FOR OUR ACHIEVEMENTS AND QUALITIES'

But you will notice that as we grow, we learn to appreciate being greatly regarded for our achievements and qualities and saddened when these attributes go undetected or are dismissed. This, my friend, is where we start to doubt the hero within and open up the possibilities for zero to enter our lives.

You were born a hero but nobody said it was going to be easy. If it was that easy, you wouldn't be reading this book.

> *"Nurture your mind with great thoughts; to believe in the heroic makes heroes"*
>
> ***Benjamin Disraeli***

Forgetting who we are

Zero *n. the lowest point.*

Like you, I was born a hero and like you, I would also forget what and who I was supposed to be and how I should behave. For many years, I lived a lesser life. A life in which I was not living, but existing. A life working towards other peoples goals and dreams. To some extent I was greatly regarded for my achievements and qualities but not by me.

This may not be your story; maybe your story goes deeper than this. An unhappy childhood, difficult teenage years, abusive or domineering parents?

Maybe you feel that you have never been greatly admired for those hero qualities or do not possess them at all. Well, you are and you do and in the chapters that follow, you will learn to appreciate those qualities in you and those around you. You will develop the characteristics of a hero and you will begin to live life as it was meant to be lived.

> *"A hero is an ordinary individual who finds the strength to persevere in spite of overwhelming obstacles"*
>
> ***Christopher Reeve***

So, where did it all go wrong and why are you reading this book?

Well, it isn't your fault. We become products of our society and our upbringing. This is not to say that our society or your parents were trying to do you any wrong. Society must learn to survive as a whole and our parents teach and prepare us to survive in this world in the only way they know how. These survival mechanisms are strong and for 'our own good'.

But in 'protecting' us from the moment of our birth, we are unwittingly held back. Told and shown how to behave and what fits in best with the beliefs, goals and aspirations of our fellow citizens. Great! But this doesn't always help us to become whole human beings or heroes.

For instance, when a young boy tells his father that he is to become a rock star! Does the father praise his son and tell him that he will be greatly regarded for his achievements and qualities and that he is already greatly regarded for his current achievement of learning to play the guitar and the quality of his personality with such drive and ambition.

Sadly, no, his father will tell him to be realistic so as to protect his son from future disappointment in a world where the odds of him becoming a rock star are so low. The first blow is struck and the boy loses a little hero from within.

This parental/social influence has been studied greatly and is now widely accepted as what is known as 'Neuro-linguistic Programming' or NLP.

NLP relates to how we as human beings are programmed (by our parents and society initially) to react and feel to certain situations.

In 'NLP for Dummies' by Romilla Ready and Kate Burton, they reflect on a similar story to that of the would-be rock star that I have just mentioned. In their story, they tell of the child who brings a self- made 'mud pie' into his mother's kitchen only to be chastised for making a mess. Of course the boy was confidently bearing a gift and his mother's reaction was not as he expected. He will now have been programmed to feel rejection, denting his confidence and helping him to forget the hero within.

Imagine how many more times this happens to you over the course of your life, once a week? Daily? Several times a day?

Think about your time at school and your work place today and I'm sure you can think of many other occasions where your qualities and achievements may have gone un-noticed or where you have purposely held back from showing those great qualities of yours for fear of the rejection and humiliation that sometimes accompanies something that you say or do.

And there we have it! You are holding back and so, are no longer being admired for your qualities and achievements – not by you, your colleagues, friends or family.

You have unwittingly 'turned off' the hero and so fit better into a society that often mocks or rejects your great qualities.

For many people this sits just fine with them. Keep your expectations low and you are never disappointed or unhappy! Or are you?

In my experience, people are rarely happy in a life where they are not recognised for their qualities and achievements. As human beings, we constantly seek the praise and approval of our peers and of ourselves.

It's no fun being ordinary, putting up with second best or under achieving, just ask your biggest critic – you!

While many people ignore the fact that they are unhappy, it is commonplace for us to replace that emptiness with food, alcohol or drug addiction.

You however: have chosen to find the hero within and enjoy the ups and downs of a real life, accepting all that goes with it!

Heroes just know

You have so far, been introduced to the negative but well intentioned efforts of individuals and our society in crushing the hero within.

This book however: is intended to inspire, motivate and help you to resuscitate that hero within and so we now take a look at those people who have been fortunate enough not to lose their hero. Those individuals 'just know' how to bring out the best in themselves and others too.
They are our heroes.

If we take another look at our parents, you will probably also remember times when a smile or simple words of encouragement made you feel a 'million dollars'.

This was a great example of those heroes bringing out the hero in you. In the same way that those same parents could give you a disapproving glance and help to destroy the hero within you.

The problem is that most people struggle at being heroes and so are little or no help in developing our hero as they give us conflicting signals through no fault of their own.

We must therefore seek out and learn from real heroes, those people in our society who always look for the 'positive' in situations and others. People who will genuinely admire you for your qualities and achievements. Most of all though, we must become real heroes ourselves.

So, where do we find these people? Firstly, I would suggest that you look at the people around you. Who do you admire for their qualities and achievements?

Maybe you only admire some of their qualities and achievements – that's ok if you recognise this.

And just to help you, I will suggest you read the books of some of my heroes: Susan Jeffers, Paul Mckenna, Norman Vincent Peale and Richard Branson to name but a few!

This list is by no means limited and I would hope that you would add many more of your own heroes to it.

You will never hear a real hero put you down. You're a dreamer, be realistic and get real are not the words of heroes. They will ask you 'why' and 'how' you intend to reach a goal. They will offer advice and support.

Following my parents, my first contact with a real hero was during a physical education lesson at secondary school. A chronic asthmatic, I could barely walk let alone run. I had the desire but nobody understood-I just couldn't breathe!

My reaction of course would be to get my parents to write a note – excusing me from physical education lessons where I would be chastised weekly by the teacher and given pages from a book to copy for the duration of the lesson.

This continued until one day, a new teacher arrived – Mr Williams! He was young, good-looking and extremely dynamic.

At the beginning of the session he took me to one side and asked why I regularly missed these sessions?

I explained and he offered a solution. His solution was to encourage me to walk where I could and 'if' I ever felt that I could run, then I should do so for a few short seconds only.

The results of this kind man's words and actions were that I began to regularly take part and believe in my self – running more and more often. Thanks to this particular hero, I now take part in regular exercise and indeed work as a personal fitness trainer!

To my knowledge, nobody told Mr Williams that he was a hero and that his treatment of me would have such a lasting effect on me and on the people that I now coach using his principles.

He just knew! He knew how to get the best out of his life and that of others around him and for those qualities and achievements I greatly admire him.

We should focus more on these kinds of people and listen less to the many unfortunate souls amongst us who for one reason or another, will always try to 'put us down'.

> *"How important it is for us to recognise and celebrate our heroes and she-roes!"*
>
> **Maya Angelou**

So real heroes just know what to say, how to act and how to feel. Or do they? Could it be that as these people were growing up, they were constantly praised and given the opportunity to fail and told that it was ok? Were they treated differently and did someone pass on the wisdom that they now possess?

Maybe! And to some extent definitely but ask a real hero why he knows and behaves the way he does and I bet he can't give you an answer. Real heroes just know.

And then there are the re-borns. People like me who have re-discovered their hero within. People who may still think and act heroically but in a conscious way. Someone you may already be, are becoming or are willing to become.

I have personally found that as time goes by and one continually acts and thinks in a certain way, it does become automatic. I therefore believe that one day when someone asks me that question, I will struggle to give him an answer and I will be a real hero.

> *"Everyone is necessarily the hero of his own life story"*
>
> ***John Barth***

To be a hero, we must heed the words of Norman Vincent Peale, Believe in yourself! Have faith in your abilities! Without a humble but reasonable confidence in your own powers you cannot be successful or happy.

So, life as an 'ordinary' person is not an option. Let's start living again.

What is our hero?

Our hero is this:

It is being greatly regarded for our qualities and achievements. It is our self- esteem, our self- belief and our ability to have, be and do anything we want.

It is helping others achieve what they want or have yet to conceive. It is living life to the fullest.

It is remembering that we must greatly regard ourselves for these qualities before we expect others to see us in the same light.

If we look at a traditional hero like 'Superman' or 'Wonder-woman', you will notice that they have certain characteristics that inspire us, and everyone around them.

They have - '**H**igh self esteem' – they believe in themselves.

They - '**E**xercise' – have great mental and physical strength.

They - '**R**adiate positivity' and we are drawn to them.

They're - '**O**rganised' – no chaos here!

H.E.R.O

Finding the 'hero within'

> *"Whatever you believe with feeling becomes your reality"*
>
> **Brian Tracy**

To find our hero again, we must take each of the characteristics of a hero and study them in a little more detail.

Remember, you already possess and may still demonstrate some or all of these characteristics but not yet realise it! If this is the case, then concentrate on the areas where you are weakest and take from this that which applies to you the most.

High Self-esteem

The Collins Gem English dictionary gives the following definition for esteem:

Vt. Think highly of; consider – n. favourable opinion, regard, respect.

Therefore, to have a high self-esteem, we must think highly of ourselves and regard ourselves in favourable opinion, treating ourselves with respect.

> *"You must love yourself before you love another. By accepting yourself and fully being what you are, your simple presence will make others happy".*
>
> ***Unknown***

When you think of someone having a high opinion of themself it will usually leave you feeling a little uncomfortable and remind you of the worst and most annoying person you know. A high self-esteem is different though. It is acknowledging that you are a decent and worthy person who deserves respect from yourself and others. This of course, is despite of your many human errors and failings.

So we must believe in ourselves. What good would it be, if in our fantasy stories, the hero turned up and questioned his own ability to fly?

We know he can fly but would lose our confidence in him and his power would be lost.

During 2008 and 2009 the world lost confidence in its banks and their ability to lend money. Although many of these banks were asset rich, several went into receivership and the 'credit crunch' was born. The world watched as we saw some of the biggest corporate losses in history.

For others to have confidence in us, we must project confidence and to project confidence, we must feel confident.

You are asset rich. By that I mean that you have a wonderful mind and body giving you the ability to achieve anything. A lack of self-belief is dangerous; it can be harmful to you and others, so start believing in yourself today.

Early in this book, we took a look at what and who may have been responsible for diminishing our hero characteristics and this may explain why your self-esteem may be lower than it should be.

They didn't try and it wasn't their fault. They didn't know what you do now. They too may have suffered with a low self-esteem and would surely have forgotten their hero within.

Blaming and focusing on negatives will not lift your spirits.

Concentrate your efforts on the heroes who made you feel good. Hold onto those moments and the Mr Williams' of this world who made you feel good and raised your self-esteem.

> *"Put all your excuses aside and remember this: YOU are capable".*
>
> ***Zig Ziglar***

Think of a time when someone gave you a reassuring glance, a compliment or praise.

Close your eyes and hold onto that thought. Turn it into a vision. Make it bigger and brighter. Focus on what you see, hear and feel. Press the thumb and middle finger of your left hand together and live that moment.

Where is your self-esteem now?

Feeling better?

And this is just your first attempt. Practice and within a short time, you will feel this way most of the time, without even trying. You will re-programme your brain to feel as good as your default setting.

This technique has been widely used and promoted by the very brilliant Mr Paul Mckenna and in his book 'Change your life in seven days', you will find more detail on these techniques along with other methods for visualising your life better.

> *"Low self-esteem is like driving through life with the hand-brake on."*
>
> **Maxwell Maltz**

Start to ease off on that brake and you are already starting to awaken the hero within you.

In the next chapter, we will look further at the steps you need to take to boost you self-esteem but for now, just be aware of what it is and what it should feel like to live life with a high self-esteem.

Exercised

When we talk about exercise, we are looking at gaining and maintaining mental and physical strength.

This second characteristic of our fictional super-hero can be visualised more easily like this:

Imagine super-guy reaching a bus full of school children, hanging precariously on a cliff's edge (he now knows that he can fly!) and realising that he doesn't have the physical strength to move the bus nor the mental strength to ask for assistance or formulate a plan of immediate action.

The bus of course would fall and the results would be disastrous.

Heroes must be strong, both mentally and physically, although either one of these attributes can become more dominant if you are overcoming some physical or mental limitations.

> *"Courage is more exhilarating than fear and in the long run it is easier. We do not have to become heroes overnight. Just a step at a time, meeting each thing that comes up, seeing it not as dreadful as it appeared, discovering we have the strength to stare it down."*
>
> *Eleanor Roosevelt*

Physical Strength

As a personal fitness trainer, for me this part is easy. For you, this may be your worst nightmare!

Our bodies are designed to work on a regular basis wherever and whenever possible. Modern living however: stops us from the very tasks we were born to do and affords us the 'luxury' of doing very little.

This, my friends, is no luxury. Asides from the decreasing ability for our bodies to perform normal tasks, we are killing ourselves slowly and most applicably to this book, we are helping to create our own low self-esteem.

How many people will tell you, that they are embarrassed by their shape or size. That they will only go on a date or take part in some activity if they lose some weight.

This may all sound very familiar, so let me be the one to tell you the way it is. If you are able bodied but overweight or lack physical fitness and do nothing about it then you will never be a true hero to yourself or anyone else.

There are no excuses and exercise does not have to be gruelling or uncomfortable. Find an activity you enjoy like walking or playing with your children. Follow a sensible diet and you will have this aspect of your life in full control in no time at all.

In fact, by reading this and deciding to do something about it, you are already making a difference.

> *"Lack of activity destroys the good condition of every human being, while movement and methodical physical exercise save it and preserve it".*
>
> ***Plato***

And what good is he who is fortunate enough to have a healthy physical body but has poor strength of mind?

Mental strength

Once you begin to treat your physical body better, you will automatically see a difference in your mental state. Good nutrition and exercise help to balance our body's natural rhythms and when you feel good about your body, it helps to lift your self-image.

In reverse, this psychosomatic behaviour will see someone in a poor state of mind, suffer with physical symptoms such as back or head ache.

In extreme cases, our mental states of high anxiety can cause some very real physical symptoms and result in panic attacks and worse.

Heroes must stand or sit up straight, shoulders back, chin up, chest out and believe in their own ability-that is mental strength.

If you are overcoming physical limitations and are unable to follow the above advice, focus on the fuel that you put into your body. Eat and sleep well and this will also have the positive effect that you desire with regard to your mental state.

Another aspect of mental strength is knowledge. How do you know – you can't do that?

Learn from reading and through experience but most of all, learn through mistakes.

Remember: That which doesn't kill us, only makes us stronger.

Radiate Positivity

We are all aware of those people who constantly moan about all of the bad things in life. How opportunities never come their way and how good luck is for other people!

To some extent you may have heard yourself using similar language from time to time.

When we view the world through negative eyes we see negative things.

Luck is what happens when the opportunities that you have been preparing for come your way and you will only see these opportunities through positive eyes.

You must be positive when everything around you is falling apart. If you can do this, you can do anything.

Heroes have high self-esteem and both physical and mental strength but these great characteristics are useless if others cannot pick up on them.

Let's think back once again to our fictional super-hero.

The bus is hanging on the cliff's edge, super-guy has strength of mind and body and confidence in his own ability but proceeds to harp on about how silly the driver must have been!

Are you drawn to our hero now? Do you admire this quality?

Of course not, he is miserable. He has amazing powers and the gift to make a massive difference in peoples lives but is focusing on the negative part of the situation in which he now finds himself.

To radiate positivity, we must count our blessings and be greatfull for all of the good things around us.

Look for the opportunities and solutions in every situation.

> **"The way we see the problem is the problem".**
>
> **Stephen Covey**

And in the words of Edward B. Butler:

"One man has enthusiasm for 30 minutes, another for 30 days, but it is the man who has it for 30 years who makes a success of his life."

The final characteristic of our hero is to be:

Organised

This is the most basic of all the characteristics but its significance must not be overlooked. You and others around you may joke about the fact that you are always late or unprepared for this or that but rest assured that you are putting yourself under greater pressure and others are having less respect for you whatever they might say.

Do you admire people who turn up late and cannot organise the simplest parts of their lives? Are they your heroes?
Take this scenario for example:

Super-guy turns up, full of self-belief, mentally and physically strong and radiating positivity but.............

He's in the wrong place! - At the wrong time! - And he's still wearing his pyjama's!

Think back to the definition of a hero. 'One who is greatly regarded for his qualities and achievements'.

If you turn up in the wrong place, at the wrong time and wearing the wrong clothes, then it is unlikely that even the most confident and positive of individuals will regard you as a hero.

> **"Don't judge a man by how he spend his weekends, but how he deals with his problems".**
>
> ***Unknown***

This final characteristic concludes our look at the qualities one must possess to truly live life as a hero and if these are qualities that you are happy to admit as your own, then congratulations. You are a hero!

If however: you require a little more help with finding parts of your hero within, then read on.

Launching the 'hero within'

Before we go any further, we must remember that nothing will ever be achieved unless we take action.

You must now decide whether to take action from the inside out or the outside in!
By this I mean that some people like to change their outward appearance and behaviour first and then work on re-programming their minds secondly as this may follow more naturally for them.

You may be the type of person who washes the outside of the car but look inside and its chaos; the oil and water levels have never been checked let alone changed.

This type of action is fine, as long as you realise that you will have to clean the inside of your life a little later on.

If you are an 'inside outer' however; then you will find the whole thing a lot easier. On first impressions you may be a little scruffy and your garden unkempt but inside both you and your home are organised and ready for change.

Both methods work and you must work with what is best for you.

> *"Conditions are never 'just right'. People who delay action until all factors are favourable, do nothing".*
>
> ***Unknown***

If we take another look at those 'hero' qualities that you already possess, we must now look to bring them out in your every day life.

Don't give up, this can and will take time and you may still have to remind yourself from time to time as you slip back into the ways of the zero!

The first quality is

'High Self-esteem'.

Remember the super Hero who didn't believe in himself?

You are a wonderful person. You can do and be anything you want to.

To launch this belief in yourself, firstly just try acting as if you have this amazing belief in your self. Work from the outside in.

Stand up tall, shoulders back and walk like you are the most successful person who has ever lived on this planet.

If you struggle with this, imagine that you are somebody else, someone you admire for his or her qualities and achievements. Try this initially for just a few minutes every day until it becomes habit and you will start to believe in yourself!

It has been said many times that you become what you do on a regular basis.

Surround yourself with people who make you feel good about yourself and avoid those people who bring you down.
Watch and read only things that inspire you and bit-by-bit little changes will begin to take place.

It really is that simple – give it a try!

The next quality is **'Exercised'**. *To be fit in mind, body and spirit.*

As a personal fitness trainer with over a decade of experience and as a person as prone to failure, depression and anxiety as anyone else, I cannot recommend exercise highly enough.

Exercise your body – if you don't like the gym, then get yourself outside and walk in the sun, wind and rain.

In many ways this type of exercise is better as even cloudy days will provide us with the essential vitamin d that we require to 'lift our mood'.

Think of exercise in the same way that you approach brushing your teeth – it's just something that we need to do each day to stop our bodies decaying.
When you exercise, you feel better physically and mentally and as a bi-product, your self-esteem will be lifted also.

Exercising the mind can and should be done by reading positive material and setting yourself tasks and goals which challenge you but are within your capabilities.

Surround yourself with the people you admire and whose conversation deepens your knowledge and problem solving ability.

Do not read the doom and gloom of our tabloid newspapers or listen to the terrible predictions of our nightly newsreaders.

Think – 'I can' and 'what's the best solution'. If it doesn't come to you, then seek out the answer from others.

The next quality is

'Radiating Positivity'.

Now that we have looked at some of the other attributes of a real hero, we must see how they put them into practise.

Having spent the time to work on your self-esteem, physical and mental strength, you will now find that you are automatically finding it easier to radiate positivity.

Next time you hear yourself joining in with a negative conversation or having those negative thoughts –

STOP!

And think – do I sound or feel like a hero?

The answer to that question will surely be no and being constantly positive can be hard.

People will still try and take advantage of you, act in negative ways towards you and try to bring you back to zero.
Try to feel compassion for such individuals, as they are most definitely at 'ground zero'. You may find it easier to avoid particularly negative individuals and that's ok too.

Give it a try- you have nothing to lose. No one ever died from looking on the bright side of life!

The final quality is **'Organised'**.

If you are to instil confidence in yourself and expect those around you to have that confidence in you, then you must be organised.

Start today. Write down whatever it is that you need to do. Add to it a time scale and take one step each day to completing what ever it is that you need to do.

Make a plan – "if you fail to plan then you plan to fail!"

Another aspect of being organised that is often overlooked, is that we tend to take on too much.

Learn to say no to people who ask for your help if it will affect the quality of the work or life that you already have. They will think more of you for this and there's always someone else to do it, no matter what they tell you.

Just imagine once again our super Hero.

How many rescues can he perform at once?

The answer is: - No more than you can.

If you get this wrong, learn from it, get back up and try again!

As we near the end of this book, let's take one more look at all of the qualities of a hero.

High in self-esteem, exercised (fit in mind body and spirit), radiating positivity and organised.

Does that sound like someone you would like to be around? Does that sound like you?

If you demonstrate these qualities then people will want to be around you and you will be at peace with yourself.

Start today. Work on the qualities that you are finding the most difficult. Seek advice and ask for feedback. Avoid the people who bring you down and surround yourself with those who lift you up.

You were born a hero – it's time to start living like one!

> **"Even if you're on the right track, you'll get run over if you just sit there"**
>
> **Will Rogers**

Super-Hero

Su'per a. inf. Very good.
Super (comb form) above, greater, exceeding(ly), as in superhu'man.

Collins Gem – English dictionary

Now that you have found or are working towards finding your hero within, why stop there?

Take another look at your heroes and she-roes. The people you admire for their qualities and achievements. Take another look at your admirable qualities and achievements also.

Do any of these qualities stand out?

Are you perhaps – 'above average' at maintaining a high self-esteem?

'Very good' at sticking to your exercise regime?

'Greater' than most people you know when it comes to radiating positivity?
Or 'exceedingly' well organised?

If you can answer 'yes' to one or more of these questions, then you have 'superhuman' qualities and are therefore a 'super-hero'.

The superhuman skills and abilities of our cartoon heroes are merely exaggerations of what ordinary people can do and achieve on a daily basis.

You are not expected to fly but achieving a pilot's license would be a 'superhuman' achievement.

Neither are you expected to be the world's strongest man or woman but sticking to an exercise regime is something that the majority of human beings cannot or do not do. This then would also render you a super-hero.

You are not expected to have a great day every day but if you can always maintain a positive outlook despite the adversity that life throws at you, then this makes you a super-hero also.

Finally and most impressively, if you have overcome or are overcoming a serious illness, been through a divorce, supported others in their time of need or suffered the loss of a loved one and can still smile or crack a joke. Are able to take a light- Hearted look at your situation and embrace the good things in your life. Then you my friend are the biggest super-hero of them all.

If you have read this far and still cannot recognise any of the super-hero qualities in yourself, then I suggest you look again.

Take a piece of paper and pen and imagine that you are someone else writing about you.

Now write down your best qualities from the outside looking in.

Do you for instance – always turn up on time?

Do you always work to the best of your abilities even if it does go unnoticed?
Are you always nice to people despite their lack of reciprocation?

These qualities and others that you can present on a continuous basis are super-hero qualities. If you are still having problems with believing that you are a super-hero, then you are 'exceedingly' humble and this is the greatest super-hero quality of them all!

> "Everyone of us excels at something, even if that something is having a tremendous lack of self belief"
>
> Author

Work on your superhuman qualities: - 'positive qualities that you can demonstrate on a consistent basis'.

Believe in yourself – this cannot and will not be emphasised enough.

If you do not believe in yourself then you will miss opportunities for fear of failure will overcome you. Therefore, you will not be able to live life as a hero or super-hero and others will find it hard to believe in you also.

Exercise regularly – maybe you will take part in and complete a physical challenge, winning a medal or just completing the distance. Maybe you will visit the gym twice this week even though you don't really feel like it! Perhaps you will exercise your mind by reading books that increase your knowledge and improve your outlook? It's up to you!

Be positive always – Life will continue to test you and sometimes the odds will seem overwhelming. Look for that glimmer of hope, that tiny light at the end of the tunnel and head towards it at break-neck speed!

We have no choice in this matter for once we 'give up' completely then we cannot achieve anything.

If you can maintain a positive outlook always – then you are a super-hero!

> *'A negative outlook never achieved a positive result'.*
>
> *Author*

Do not rule out spontaneity though as this is the spice of life. To have room for spontaneous acts in such a chaotic life, we must first be organised.

To put it simply and as my mother used to say: - 'you can play when your chores are done'.

Get your chores done now! – 'playing' is much more fun when you know that you don't have a huge pile of ironing or bills that need paying waiting for you when you get back home.

This, more than anything, will drastically reduce the stresses in your day-to-day life and give your self-esteem a good kick in the right direction.

Take action – do something towards organising your life now!

Follow this advice and if you're not already a super-hero –

YOU WILL BE!

Super-heroes
Are
Unconditionally
Predisposed to success,
Exceed at something
Regularly,

Have

High self-esteem,
Exercise
Radiate positiviy
And are
Organised

A brief trip back to zero

Zero n. the lowest point

So what exactly is zero?

According to our dictionaries definition, it is quite simply the 'lowest point'.

This point at which, you may have now reached or have been at some point in your life.

For you, this may be that you are now or have been at the heaviest weight that you have ever been in your life?

You may be suffering a loss, recently divorced or totally lacking in control in some or all areas of your life?

Well, the good thing about reaching the bottom is that there is only one way to go and that is up!

Sometimes in our lives, we have to visit zero in order to stand back, evaluate our situation and formulate a plan of action. It can and should be viewed as a good thing.

You may have heard yourself or other people commenting that if it were not for their personal tragedies, then they would never have changed their job or visited somewhere new or taken the risks that brought about their greatest rewards.

If and when you visit 'zero' next, be thankful and think – what opportunities will come from this and how can I adapt my behavior to deal with things better in the future.

Hopefully you are now feeling inspired and are ready to take action and work on the 'Hero' qualities that need the most work.

Perhaps you already take physical exercise but are disorganised?

Perhaps you are organised but lack the self-Belief to take action?

Whatever it is, we all feel this way from time to time and you must not let it become the way you are. It is the way you were.

In the past, you may have avoided taking action because you lacked belief in yourself or had not yet practiced or honed the five qualities that bring out the hero in you.

Work on these qualities every day. Read back through this book whenever you need a little 'pick me up'.

Surround yourself with other 'Heroes' and you will find that you automatically begin to behave like one.

I have been back to zero many times and whenever one or more of my qualities seems to lack a little polish, I return to the inspiration of my hero's. Many of these hero's are authors of motivational books and cd's and some are simply the people around me who I can admire. My wife, my children, some colleagues, my parents, brothers, sisters and in-laws all have particular qualities that I admire.

They are my heroes.

Remember, it is your ability to overcome adversity despite your many failings and weakness as a human being that makes you a hero.

If you have physical limitations, then you will notice how you are able to focus on your mental strength. A great example of this is a colleague of mine who was seriously injured in a road accident as a young boy but never fails to make me laugh. His physical limitations have been far surpassed by his brilliant sense of humour.

I have also known many people who suffer with depression and are unable to deal with everyday tasks but somehow drag themselves off to complete a physical challenge that only the bravest of souls would even contemplate. These people have found that although they may have mental limitations, their physical abilities have doubled in strength.

These heroes will also touch ground zero from time to time but it's the ability to get back up, dust themselves off and start again that makes them true heroes.

The author's story

Lying awake at four o clock in the morning, staring up at the ceiling, I am wondering how my life has ever come to this.

My wife is almost nine months pregnant with our second child.

I am nervous about the birth, the future for my children and I can't sleep. Work is getting me down, I'm low in self-esteem, my exercise regime is suffering badly, I'm anything but positive and totally disorganised!

Insomnia is good for one thing however; you have time to work out your problems and concerns and find the solutions for those problems.

My solution is this book! I had plenty of time to contemplate how my life had come to this, the qualities that I would like to demonstrate to my wife, my children and myself. The qualities that I would like my children to posses, in order to live the most fulfilling lives that they could lead.

The solutions that I came up with that night have been both eye opening and practical and have improved the lives of everyone around me.

Like you, I have had many ups and downs in my life and I'm sure that there will be many more to come.

The difference now is that I am my own hero. I believe in myself and my abilities to deal with whatever life throws at me.

I was born a hero and now I'm acting like one!

My background is nothing too unusual either. I am the fourth child of six, born to two loving parents in the 1970's.

I was an average pupil at school, well behaved but with the usual boisterous tendencies. I excelled only in art but was always keen to win my teachers approval in all subjects.

A love of all things physical was limited slightly by my lack of ability to breathe but despite this, I would do well at many of the sports day events during my primary school years. Later, I would regularly drop out of physical education lessons during my time at secondary school but was rescued by a hero and to this day, I am an exercise fanatic!

My family are fairly close but busy work schedules and distance- keep us apart more than I would like. Each of us though, is aware that we are never more than a phone call away.

Home-life for me now is both challenging and rewarding. As I write this page, my second daughter has reached five months of age and is definitely a hero in her own right. She confidently lets us know what she wants and we can't admire everything she does enough!

My eldest daughter, now in her eighth year, is blossoming with confidence. She is achieving new skills on a daily basis but is humble when it comes to the attention she receives for doing so. She is most definitely a hero also.

Last but not least, my wife. This wonderful woman who puts up with me, and all of my idiosyncrasies – she would have to be a hero to do that now wouldn't she!!

www.ingramcontent.com/pod-product-compliance
Lightning Source LLC
Chambersburg PA
CBHW031415040426
42444CB00005B/579